T0113897

THIRTY LETTERS
OF
DEVOTION

A Journal for the Christian Soul

L. M. LEWIS

WESTBOW
PRESS®
A DIVISION OF THOMAS NELSON
& ZONDERVAN

This book is a work of non-fiction. Unless otherwise noted, the author and the publisher make no explicit guarantees as to the accuracy of the information contained in this book and in some cases, names of people and places have been altered to protect their privacy.

WestBow Press books may be ordered through booksellers or by contacting:

WestBow Press
A Division of Thomas Nelson & Zondervan
1663 Liberty Drive
Bloomington, IN 47403
www.westbowpress.com
844-714-3454

Because of the dynamic nature of the Internet, any web addresses or links contained in this book may have changed since publication and may no longer be valid. The views expressed in this work are solely those of the author and do not necessarily reflect the views of the publisher, and the publisher hereby disclaims any responsibility for them.

Any people depicted in stock imagery provided by Getty Images are models, and such images are being used for illustrative purposes only. Certain stock imagery © Getty Images.

Scripture taken from the King James Version of the Bible.

ISBN: 978-1-6642-4769-7 (sc)
ISBN: 978-1-6642-4768-0 (e)

Print information available on the last page.

WestBow Press rev. date: 04/22/2022

DEDICATION

This book is dedicated to my dear Aunt Susan a true Christian. Gone too soon, but forever in my heart.

This book is also dedicated to my Apostle, Preston Davis Jr. and his lovely wife Pastor Chiquetta Davis along with the True Love Church International family located in North Carolina. Thanks for holding me accountable to the word of God and pushing me to be a true disciple of Christ. Words cannot express my love and appreciation for having Shepherds after God's own heart and a body of believers whose iron sharpens iron. I love you all.

A LETTER TO THE READERS AND WRITERS

Dear Brothers and Sisters in Christ,

Being a follower of Christ is a wonderful and lifelong journey. The journey has many mountain top experiences and several valley experiences, but each experience has a distinct purpose. The purpose may be for spiritual growth, to learn obedience or to master the love walk. Whatever the experience we know that all things will work together for the good of those who love Christ (Romans 8:28). As you read each devotional letter of encouragement, inspiration, or admonition, think about a time you found yourself in a similar situation. Pen your thoughts about it in a letter to God. Tell him what you learned from reading the letter and how you can apply the scripture references into your daily life. The letters in this journal come from various times in my life when I totally surrendered my life to God. I hope these letters will inspire you and give you hope as you work out your own soul salvation (Philippians 2:12).

Sincerely,

L.M. Lewis

CONTENTS

DAY 1

The Place

Dear Brothers and Sisters in Christ,

Has anyone ever looked at you when you went into a place that your social status or background made it **APPEAR** that you shouldn't be there? Well, I came to tell you that the word in the book of Proverbs 18:16 tells us that a man's gift will make room for him and bring him before great men. So, don't fret when people look at you as if you don't belong. Your gift got you there. The Jews in the Synoptic Gospels of Matthew, Mark, Luke and John never received the full benefits of having Christ right here on earth. They looked at him as a carpenter's son rather than for the gift he really was. People look at the exterior of a person or what they know of the person rather than the gift that they truly are. Just keep showing up at those places. Your gift put you there and it will make room for you.

Yours Truly

Write a letter to God telling him about a time you felt displaced or felt you didn't belong and how you are going to replace those negative feelings with what he says about you.

Scriptures to reference

Jeremiah 29:11, 1 Peter 2:9, Galatians 3:29, Psalm 139:14

Date: _____

Dear God,

_____

_____

_____

_____

_____

_____

_____

_____

_____

_____

_____

_____

DAY 2

The Foolish Heart

Dear Brothers and Sisters in Christ,

Who can know their own heart? Who can know someone else's heart? The songwriter Steve Perry touched the surface in the 80's with the song "Foolish Heart" but the prophet Jeremiah explained the problem with the heart. Jeremiah 17:9 tells us that the heart is deceitful and desperately wicked, who can know it. Know that our hearts can deceive us. Have you ever heard the saying, "Follow your Heart?"

We must be careful with following our hearts because our hearts can deceive us. This is certainly true when it comes to love and romance. People fall in love with the wrong people all the time because their heart wanted what they thought was love but it was just lust. Love and romance are just one example, however there are other areas in our lives that can fall prey to this deceitful heart. The ways we think are right based on the feelings in our heart can lead to our own demise (Proverbs 14:12).

But there is an antidote. If we acknowledge God first with all of our decisions, he will direct us down the right path. As Christians we are not to rely on our hearts, but we are to rely totally on God to help us make the right decisions and choices for our lives.

Who wants to be deceived by their own heart? Proverbs 4:23 tells us to guard our hearts because out of it are the issues of life. We do not truly know our hearts, but God does. He is the only one who can deal with the heart effectively.

That is why there is so much emphasis in the bible on getting our hearts right. Once your heart gets right, hearing and distinguishing between the voice of your heart and the voice of God becomes apparent. Then you can have the assurance that you will not fall victim to the foolish heart.

Sincerely Yours

Write a letter to God telling him about a time that you followed your heart and the results were undesirable. Tell him your plans on how you are going to apply the word of acknowledging him first before making any decisions.

Scriptures to reference

Proverbs 3:5, Proverbs 4:23, Psalm 51:10, Psalm 26:2

Date: _____

Dear God,

_____

_____

_____

_____

_____

_____

_____

_____

_____

_____

_____

DAY 3

Let's Go Fishing

Dear Brothers and Sisters in Christ,

You have surrendered your life to Christ and have made the choice to lay down your life and live for him. With that being said, let's go fishing. What do I mean? Let's catch others with our walk. Let's live righteous even when the opportunity to live unrighteous is ever present. Let's walk in love even when wrath is justified. Of course, it is easier said than done. To live the Christ centered life, we must totally surrender our thoughts, desires and actions to God and follow what he says in spite of our rebellious flesh. When we give up our ungodly lifestyle that is when we can truly win souls for Christ. In doing so, the unbeliever will see our good works and glorify our Lord and Savior Jesus Christ. People will want to be like us because they see us go through trials and still have hope. They see our beginnings and notice that our latter is better. They notice our joy even though our circumstances are less than perfect. They see us withstand the hardness of people without letting corrupt communication come out of our mouths. The unbeliever will see the difference between us and themselves and they will want what we have. They will see, rather than be told Greater is he that is in you than he that is in the world. So, let's get ready like a fisherman to fish. Let's get our bait ready which is a righteous lifestyle. Let's get our nets ready by being intentional with our walk with God. Now get your pole, aim, and launch. Get ready for the people you are going to bring to Christ. Are you ready? Let's go fishing.

Warm Wishes

Write a letter to God telling him how you need his help to bring your flesh under total submission to him. Let him know that you are serious and intentional about winning souls for hm by proving that Greater is he that is in you, than he that is in the world.

Scriptures to reference

Luke 5:10, 1 John 4:4, Romans12:2, 2 Corinthians 5:17

Date: _____

Dear God,

_____

_____

_____

_____

_____

_____

_____

_____

_____

_____

_____

DAY 4

What's in Your Storage Room?

Dear Brothers and Sisters in Christ,

We all know that material things come and go. Believe me I have had my share of loss. But there was a time back in 2016 when a hurricane swept through North Carolina and the losses were devastating. A natural disaster is a real eye opener to what is and what is not important. I saw people with lovely homes loaded with everything that money could buy lose all of it in a matter of hours. It was then that a familiar scripture came to mind. The scripture says do not store up for yourselves treasures on this earth which moth and rust do destroy and thieves break in and steal, but rather store up for yourselves treasures in heaven that moth and rust do not destroy and thieves do not break in and steal (Matthew 6:19-21). What are those things that thieves cannot break in and steal, nor moth and rust cannot destroy? Thieves cannot steal things that are of a spiritual matter, things like agape love for our families, brothers and sisters, forgiveness and restoration for the ones who have wronged us, goodness, mercy, longsuffering, forbearance, kindness these are tangible things that no one can steal. These things will fill up our treasure boxes in heaven. Why not start today? Store up things that our God has freely given to us because we have surrendered our lives to him. And when we store up those things' others can freely receive the same treasure we have freely received. The treasure of salvation and the spiritual benefits thereof.

Best Regards

Write a letter to God telling him that you will be mindful not to be so concerned with material creations and more concerned about the things of a spiritual matter as you walk with him.

Scriptures to reference

Matthew 6: 19-21, Matthew 6:33, Galatians 5:22, Mark 4:19

Date: _____

Dear God,

_____

_____

_____

_____

_____

_____

_____

_____

_____

_____

_____

DAY 5

Prayers and Righteousness

Dear Brothers and Sisters in Christ,

One of the most powerful tools and weapons that we have available to us is prayer. Prayer is our way to communicate directly with God. It is a way for us to let him know our needs, desires, problems and to stand in intercession for others. Prayer is also a way to communicate our adoration of God and our gratefulness to him for not allowing us to die in our sin. With that being conveyed, do you know some prayers may not be answered. If a prayer is not answered; it could be a prayer that does not line up with the word of God, it was selfish, or we were not prepared for it. But there is another reason why prayers are not answered. The reason is disobedience to God's word. A very popular scripture reads that the effectual fervent prayer of a righteous man avails much (James 5:16). This simply means that if a person is living their life according to the commands of God, it is a sure thing that their prayers will be answered. However, on the other hand if you are not living right, you are double minded. You say you are a Christian and your mouth praises God, but your lifestyle cannot be distinguished as different from that of the unbeliever. You have two lifestyles and the bible states that a double minded man will receive nothing of the lord (James 1:6-8). The scripture refers to someone who doubts God, but if you are living for God and the world too you are doubleminded in your actions. How can God answer a prayer for someone who is not living according to his will? If we want our prayers to be answered much, we must be in right standing with God. It pleases him to answer our prayers because we glorify him and prove that he is a man of his word. Now I am not saying that your prayers will be answered right away all the time, but I do know for sure that it will be answered at the right time. When you pray and you are living righteously you can count on your prayer being answered if it lines up with the will of God. But if you are living two lives it is very likely that your prayers will not be answered. Live righteous, pray and your prayer life will flourish because your prayers will be answered much.

Sincerely Yours

Write a letter to God telling how you intend on getting into his word and study to learn how to live according to his word. Let him know that you are going to put action behind your words and begin to live righteous. Remind him that when you live righteous that your prayers will be answered much.

*** Scriptures to reference ***

James 5:16, James 1:8, Nehemiah 1:10-11

Date: _____

Dear God,

_____

_____

_____

_____

_____

_____

_____

_____

_____

_____

_____

_____

DAY 6

The Rule of 100

Dear Brothers and Sisters in Christ,

I'm not here to discredit the 80/20 rule. I am her to testify about the 100/100 rule. Love thy God with all your heart, all your soul and all your strength (Deuteronomy 6:5). Seek his righteousness first and all the things you need or seek will be added unto you (Matthew6:33). My God shall supply all your need according to his riches and glory (Philippians 4:19). Give God your all and he will give you everything you need. Rather than settle for 80, love the Lord and gain your 100.

I want to emphasize on Matthew 6:33. It tells us to seek the kingdom of God and his righteousness, and all these things will be added unto us. What is in the kingdom? The kingdom has everything that is needed to walk into the fullness of Christian living. Once we seek the things of a spiritual nature and walk in them, the natural things that we seek will come. 2 Peter 1:3 tells us that God gives us everything we need for life and for holy living. He gives it through his great power. As we come to know him better, we learn that He called us to share his glory and perfect life. Doesn't that sound like 100 percent of what you need. Sometimes we look to people to fill the void or empty areas in our lives, but man was not equipped to do that. If man was equipped to do that, we would not need a Savior. We must look to hills from whence cometh our help. The Psalmist told us that all or our help comes from the Lord (Psalm 121:1). The key word is all. Once we look to the hills all we need is ready and waiting for us. I repeat seek the Lord and gain your 100.

Be Encouraged

Write a letter to God telling him how you will make a conscious effort to seek his kingdom and his righteousness. Let him know that you will be more concerned with building his kingdom by living a righteous life.

*** Scriptures to reference ***

Matthew 6:33, Philippians 4:19, 3John 2:2

Date: _____

Dear God,

_____

_____

_____

_____

_____

_____

_____

_____

_____

_____

_____

_____

DAY 7

Facts and Truth

Dear Brothers and Sisters in Christ,

What is a fact? A fact is a natural law, concept or thing that is proven to be true in any situation, time, or place. Facts are or should be common knowledge to anyone. The world makes decisions, transactions, and exchanges, based on facts that are seen in the natural. But did you know that there are spiritual truths that supersede natural laws? Yes, facts are true and can be proven, but spiritual truths will override any natural fact. You may have cancer and that is a fact, but the spiritual truth is that by the stripes of Jesus you are healed (Isaiah 53:5). If you believe the truth and walk in it, it will manifest, and that fact becomes null and void. It could very well be a fact that your bank account is empty and there seems to be no way to make ends meet. But the truth is that God shall supply all your needs according to his riches and glory (Philippians 4:19). I once wrote out my monthly budget and according to that budget I did not make enough to cover my expenses. But as I began to ponder on my expenses, I realized that no bill ever went unpaid and everything I needed I had. And often, I had extra to purchase things I wanted. As the Psalmist said, I have been young and I have been old, but I have never seen the righteous forsaken or his seed begging bread (Psalm37:25). God was and still is my supplier. See God's truth will override a fact anytime. All we have to do is believe. Remember, God watches over his word to perform it (Jeremiah 1:12). Speak the word, believe it and if you believe it, you will live it. And when you live it, it will manifest.

All Praises to the Living God

Write a letter to God thanking him for his word that is true. Tell him how you plan to believe his word that pertains to your situation rather than focusing on the fact. Let him know that you believe his word above all facts because his word is true.

Scriptures to reference

Psalm 37:25, Luke 17:14, Isaiah 53:5, Philippians 4:19

Date: _____

Dear God,

_____

_____

_____

_____

_____

_____

_____

_____

_____

_____

_____

_____

DAY 8

Pit Perfect

Dear Brothers and Sisters in Christ,

Have you read the story of Joseph? If you read it, you know about the pit that he was thrown in. The pit was not a pretty place. It was dark and empty. Joseph probably thought he would die. Have you ever felt like you were in a dark and empty place? Were there life situations in which you felt death was your only way out? If so, you were in one of the many pits of life. Could you ever imagine that some of the pits orchestrated by people, circumstances or our own fault could be turned around for our good. The pit of grief, the pit of depression, the pit of drug addiction and the list goes on and on. Some individuals find their purpose when they come out of the pit. Once they come out of the pit, they save many people alive, just like Joseph did. Joseph went through several other trials after coming out of the pit, but the pit prepared him from it. See Joseph was perfect for the pit because when he came out, he found his purpose which was to come up with a plan to save people from death during a famine. Joseph was the only one fit for the pit that he found himself in because God knew it would turn out for good. Everyone could not have endured that pit. Everyone cannot endure some of life's pits that we have found ourselves in. The experiences that we had in our pits will help us to minister and help others come out of the same pit that we were once in. We should be grateful for the pits of life. The glory comes when we get out.

Warm Regards

Write a letter to God in which you share the emotions you felt in some of the pits of life. Let him know that you will not always look at the pit as a place of sorrow, but a place where spiritual growth can take place. Tell him how you plan to use your experiences in the pits of life to minister to others and give them hope as well while going through a pit of life.

Scriptures to reference

Genesis 37-50:20, James 1:2-8, Romans 5:3, 1Peter 4:12

Date: _____

Dear God,

_____

_____

_____

_____

_____

_____

_____

_____

_____

_____

_____

_____

DAY 9

An Intentional Love

Dear Brothers and Sisters in Christ,

Did you know that there are many definitions for love? Most are of an emotional act of affection for an individual, location or activity. But for the Christian, love goes far beyond the scholarly definitions of desire and affection. For the Christian love not only fulfills the entire law, but it solidifies our love for God. The New Testament tells us that God so loved the world that he gave us his only son. Jesus, God's only son came to teach the world how to love one another and the God that we serve.

In these latter days, God extends grace to us coupled with his mercy that gives us time to learn and adhere to his word. Adhering to the words from the heart of God represents our love for him. Jesus said, if possible, let this cup pass as he was on his way to the cross (Matthew 26:39). However, he was obedient. He also loved God's people. He knew that his death would give life to so many. Therefore, he disregarded his own life to save others. The bible tells us that there is no greater love than this: that a person would lay down their life for the sake of his friends (John 15:13). Now that is love.

Loving others is a fulfillment of the law because in love there is no sin. This kind of love allows us to love people that are less than loveable and not to seek our own. The kind of love I'm talking about is that agape love. The love that gives us the ability to love even if it is not reciprocated. Agape love withstands hate, betrayal, gossip, lies and even our own feelings, because we know that in the end love will win. This kind of love is purposed to overcome all evil.

Love is an act of putting others before ourselves, no matter the cost. To display that kind of love it must be intentional. This kind of love comes with a price, but your labor of love will not go unrewarded.

P.S. I Love You

Write a letter to God explaining to him how you will put an emphasis on walking in love daily. Let him know that you desire to love him because if you love him you will see others the way he sees them. Let him know that the love he freely gave will freely be given to those around you.

Scriptures to reference

Matthew 5: 43-48, John 3:16, Romans 5:8, 1 John 4:7-9 1Corinthians 13: 4-8

Date: _____

Dear God,

_____

_____

_____

_____

_____

_____

_____

_____

_____

_____

_____

_____

DAY 10

A Call to Obedience

Dear Brothers and Sisters in Christ,

Before we received salvation, we were obedient to our sin nature. The bible tells us that we were born in sin and shaped in iniquity. Therefore, we conducted ourselves in the ways of the world in which we were born. However, when we received salvation, we were born again and in this new birth we received a new way of living. The new way of living is totally opposite to the old way of life for us. We now have a new set of rules to live by. In our former lives we lived according to the will of our flesh whether wrong or right. This new way of living requires us to deny our flesh and live according to the statutes in the bible. Our old way of living was in the way of darkness, but the new way of living is the way of light. To live in the light, we have to be a light. To do that, we obey God's word. All God's commands and instructions are in the bible. The bible instructs us to pray for our enemies, so we must do it. It is totally different from the old way of life. The old way of life would tell us to hate our enemies and get even with them. The bible instructs us to flee sexual immorality. If we want to please God, we need to do it not matter how we feel. That is totally opposite, because under the old way of living it is okay to do whatever makes us feel good, but to live the Christian life it is not so. We are obedient to the word of God no matter how our flesh feels. When we got saved, we proclaimed our love for God. How do we prove that love? We prove it by being obedient to his word. The bible tells us that if we love God, then we will keep his commandments (John 14:15).

Live the Word

Write a letter to God telling him how you will put his word into practice by being obedient. Let him know that today you are making a conscious decision to live in the light of his word in obedience.

Scriptures to reference

Matthew 4:4, John 15:14, 2 John 1:6, Psalm 119:60

Date: _____

Dear God,

_____

_____

_____

_____

_____

_____

_____

_____

_____

_____

_____

DAY 11

Searching for a Healer

Dear Brothers and Sisters in Christ,

Was there ever a time in your life when you were sick physically or emotionally? Most of the time when we are sick or wounded, we go to our family physician or seek some type of medical care. But what do we do for those internal hurts and wounds? Some seek counseling while others turn to their vices or to self-destructive behavior in order to receive some type of relief from the pain inside. Some people drink heavily or turn to substance abuse, while others are promiscuous with their flesh. Then there are the few who commit violent acts against others. The commonality of all these behaviors is that they give temporary relief from the pain and the outcome is the same. The majority are back at square one or worse off than they were before the pain. That is why it is so important for us Christians to know what is available to us. We have a healer, and his name is Jesus. If you want to be healed, don't look for healing in your own strength, look to the healer. God sent his word to heal (Psalm 107:20), and he also sent his son Jesus to heal us if we only believe. We can be reminded of the account of the blind man named Bartimaeus who sat on the roadside begging who heard Jesus passing by (Mark 10:46- 47). He cried out until Jesus called him and asked him what it was, he wanted. Bartimaeus asked for his sight and Jesus told him to go his way because his faith had made him whole. He received his sight immediately (Mark 10:52). All Bartimaeus had to do was believe and he was healed. I challenge you today to call on the healer. Tell him what you need to be healed of. Believe, and you will be healed.

All Praises to the Most High

Write a letter to God telling him about a time you looked to other sources for healing. Let him know that you will no longer look to yourself or anything outside of him for your healing. Tell him that you believe he sent his word to heal and that by the stripes of Jesus you are healed.

Scriptures to reference

2 Kings 20:5, Jeremiah 30:17, Psalm 107:20-21

Mark 10: 51-52

Date: _____

Dear God,

_____

_____

_____

_____

_____

_____

_____

_____

_____

_____

_____

DAY 12

Who Are You Fighting?

Dear Brothers and Sisters in Christ,

Once we got saved, we entered a battlefield. We had several enemies. Our flesh and its vices. We also inherited Satan and rulers of wickedness in high places. They are our number one enemy. As time went on, we realized that to fight our enemies we had to apply the word of God and be prepared daily with our spiritual armor. We quickly learned that our flesh can be rebellious and easily tempted. We found out that Satan wants to make war with us just because we are living right. In this case, we learned to war in the spirit to get a prayer answered. God is pleased with us when we stick to his word even in the face of various temptations and tribulations. But what happens to us when we begin to give in to our fleshly desires or yield to the temptations that Satan presents to us. When this happens; we are fighting a whole other enemy; God. He becomes our enemy and who can stand before the living God. If we call ourselves Christians and disregard the words that God has commanded us to live by, he becomes our enemy. If you read the bible, you will notice that anyone God destroyed was deliberately disobedient to his word. On the other hand, we will also notice that Satan only went after people who were living right. He went after Job a just and upright man; he went after Jesus the Savior of the world and the Apostles of old because they were spreading the gospel and winning souls to Christ. Sometimes we think we are fighting Satan when in actuality we are being resisted by an angry God. To determine who, we are fighting we need to analyze ourselves. We must ask ourselves are we being obedient to the word of God or yielding to our flesh and various temptations? If we are yielding to our flesh; we repent (sin no more) and get back in right standing with God. When our ways please the Lord even our enemies are at peace with us (Proverbs 16:7). Now if we are being obedient and have brought our flesh under submission and find ourselves in tribulation, we don't have to worry. In this since we know that God will restore back to us anything Satan has stolen. I call us believers to examine ourselves daily to make sure we are living according to the will of God. It is a sure proclamation, that no one wants God as an enemy.

Prayerfully Yours

Write a letter to God in which you repent for the times when you deliberately disobeyed his word and yielded to your own vices or allowed yourself to be swayed away from your faith by the devices of Satan. Let him know that you will be obedient to him and follow his righteousness.

Scriptures to reference

James 4:6, Romans 1:18, Hebrews 10:26-31, 1 John 4:4

Date: _____

Dear God,

_____

_____

_____

_____

_____

_____

_____

_____

_____

_____

_____

_____

_____

_____

DAY 13

A Call to Suffer

Dear Brothers and Sisters in Christ,

Do you want to glorify God? If so, you can with your testimony and your righteous lifestyle. However, there is another way to glorify God that is not pleasing to the flesh. Suffering for the gospel's sake is another way to glorify God. We all know that sometimes we go through trials and tribulations that test our faith. In these situations, we must be steadfast and unmovable because we know that God will bring us through and out of the trial at the right time. Although we partake in the glory of Christ we must also partake in his suffering, for it is in the suffering that God is glorified. The whole purpose of suffering is to prove that we are faithful to the word of God even though things in our lives are less than perfect. Remember Job. He suffered to prove that his love for God and his faith would not fail even though he experienced great loss. What better way to prove to a lost and dying world that God is real and that the hope that we have cannot be shaken even in adverse situations. Christ suffered on several occasions, but in the end, he glorified God. The Gospel is now preached all over the world and the name of Jesus is celebrated throughout the earth. Talk about glory. When the unbeliever sees us in a trial, and we do not waiver in our faith or throw in the towel they begin to wonder what is different about us. They begin to wonder how we can still have hope in some of the most hopeless situations. That is the perfect time to tell them the good news. The unbeliever will be more prone to listen to the good news when he or she sees us living by the word even though the opportunity to give in is present. The unbeliever only knows the human response to suffering, but to see a spiritual response to suffering is foolishness to them but they will know that God is in the midst. Therefore, they will give God glory and it is our hope that he or she will be converted. So, my fellow Christians, think it not strange when you go through various trials and tribulations but be glad. For in your suffering, you have an opportunity to glorify God.

Joyfully Yours

Write a letter to God telling him that you will no longer become discouraged while going through a trial. Tell him that you will thank him for the opportunity to bring glory to his name.

Scriptures to reference

1Peter 4: 12-14, 1 Peter 5:10, 2 Corinthians 4:17

Date: _____

Dear God,

_____

_____

_____

_____

_____

_____

_____

_____

_____

_____

_____

_____

_____

DAY 14

Lose Yourself

Dear Brothers and Sisters in Christ,

In the book of Matthew 10:39, Jesus is teaching his disciples and he tells them that he who finds his life shall lose it and he that loses his life for my sake shall find it. What does that mean? It means we must lose the way of life we had before salvation and come into the new life that is now set before us. This new life is a life of holiness and righteous living. A life that is now dependent upon God and not our own independent will. Before salvation we lived the lives, we wanted. We said whatever we wanted, did whatever we wanted according to our own desires and perceptions.

However, salvation presents us a with a whole new outlook on living. This life requires us to give up our will, our way of thinking and lifestyle that is not aligned to biblical statutes. 2 Corinthians 5:17 tells us that if any many be in Christ, he is a new creature, old things have passed away, behold all things become new. As a believer, we respond to situations differently than we did before. Instead of cursing, we bless, instead of lying, we speak the truth, instead of backbiting we pray for others. We live in a totally different way and that requires us to lose ourselves. When we lose ourselves, we find our new life in him. The old sin nature of living leads to death, but the way of the righteous is eternal life in Christ Jesus. So, it is a wonderful thing to lose yourself to find your new life in him.

What a Wonder is He

Write a letter to God asking him to guide you as you begin to lose your current life to find your new life in him. Let him know that you are willing to lose whatever it is that is deterring you from totally living your new life in him.

Scriptures to reference

Matthew 10:39, 2Corinthians 5:17, Matthew 25:46, Romans 6:23

Date: _____

Dear God,

_____

_____

_____

_____

_____

_____

_____

_____

_____

_____

_____

_____

DAY 15

A Time to Celebrate

Dear Brothers and Sisters in Christ,

Resurrection Sunday or some call it Easter, is the time of year when we Christians celebrate Jesus the risen Savior. When most of us were kids our parents would buy us a new outfit and the entire family would go to church. Afterwards there was usually a feast directly after service. However, in thinking about this time of year we can be reminded of Luke chapter 23. In this chapter, Jesus is sent to Pilate before embarking on the journey up Golgotha Hill. Pilate not finding any fault in him immediately sent him to Herod who had heard many things about Jesus and had hoped to see a miracle himself. Therefore, he asked Jesus many questions, but Jesus did not respond. Herod not knowing what else to do sent Jesus back to Pilate in an expensive robe after he and his men had finished mocking him. Take notice though, Herod and Pilate were known enemies but an encounter with Christ made them friends at once. Upon the return of Jesus, Pilate plead with the chief priest and rulers of the Jews telling them that there was no reason for Jesus to be put to death. But they insisted Jesus be crucified and begged for the release of Barabbas a known murderer. Now the bible does not tell us anything about Barabbas or how he lived his life after being set free. What will we do now that we are free? We as Christians should ponder on our lives and how we were guilty of sin, but Jesus was willing to give his life so that all mankind could be free from the curse of sin and death. Just as Barabbas was guilty as charged, so were we. But Jesus took our place. We can stand in awe of our Savior who was willing to lay down his life for the guilty so they could go free. I ask again, what will we do with our new freedom? We can begin by writing a new life story in which we live our lives for him. The life that he so selflessly gave for you and me. Pilate's ONE encounter with Jesus made he and Herod friends, and the sacrifice of ONE man, Jesus gave life to many. Let's celebrate his life.

God Bless

Write a letter to God thanking him for the sacrifice Jesus made for you. Explain to him your plans for walking and living in your new-found freedom in him.

Scriptures to reference

Luke 23, Mark 15: 1-15, John 18: 28-40

Date: _____

Dear God,

_____

_____

_____

_____

_____

_____

_____

_____

_____

_____

_____

_____

_____

_____

_____

DAY 16

A Remedy for Jealousy

Dear Brothers and Sisters in Christ,

I am going to ask an honest question. Were you ever jealous of someone because of looks, what they had or their lifestyle? If so, you were subconsciously wanting to be them. We oftentimes find ourselves looking at others and wishing we were in their shoes, but we really don't know what is going on in their lives behind the scenes. When we are jealous, we are also breaking a commandment. The commandment that tells us not to covet anything that our neighbor has (Exodus 20:17). In all honesty everything on this earth belongs to God and if we are his we have access to everything he owns. Now there are qualifications to receive the blessings of God, just know you have access to it. However, there is a remedy for jealousy. Instead of looking at others and secretly wanting to be them or have what they have look to Jesus. Desire to be like him and desire to have what he has and has freely given. If we do this, we will be like the greatest human being that ever walked on this earth. If we spend our time working towards looking like Jesus, we won't have time to be jealous of anyone because we will be so focused on becoming more like Jesus.

Truthfully Yours

Write a letter to God and tell him about a time you were jealous or wished you had what someone else had. Tell him that you know it is a sin to be jealous and that you repent and intend on looking to him instead of others to fulfill the longing in your soul.

Scriptures to reference

Exodus 20:17, Ephesians 5:5, Colossians 3:5

Date: _____

Dear Christian,

_____

_____

_____

_____

_____

_____

_____

_____

_____

_____

_____

_____

DAY 17

Let Your Enemies Be

Dear Brothers and Sisters in Christ,

We all have encountered an enemy from time to time. Enemies are there to hinder us from fulfilling our purpose or teach us lessons which catapult our Christian growth. We all know that we have spiritual enemies in high places. Those spiritual enemies influence people to hate us or do evil things to us. Naturally speaking we want to get even or do something to let our enemies know that we are on to what they are doing. However, as a Christian, we must let our enemies be. God is the only one that has the right to administer wrath to our enemies. Our job is to love our enemies. There is nowhere in the New Testament that God gives us the right to administer punishment to others who have wronged us. It is his job and his job alone. He has it covered.

1. He will prepare a table before us right in front of our enemies (Psalm 23:5).
2. Vengeance is his: He will avenge us (Romans 12:19).
3. God is not mocked: Our enemies will reap what they sow just like everyone else (Galatians 6:7).
4. God becomes and enemy to our enemies (Exodus 23:22).
5. When the enemy comes in like a flood, God will raise up a standard against them (Isaiah 59:19).

Now you don't have to take my word for it. Take the time to read about how God handled the enemies of Moses. Be blessed my brothers and sisters.

Let Your Enemies Be

Write a letter to God telling him about a time when you sought out your enemies. Let him know that you will no longer try to fight your enemies in your own strength. Explain to him how you will now leave your enemies in his hands because he is the only one with the authority to administer wrath.

Scriptures to reference

Romans 12:19, Deuteronomy 32:5, Hebrews 10:30, Leviticus 19:18

Date: _____

Dear God,

_____

_____

_____

_____

_____

_____

_____

_____

_____

_____

_____

_____

DAY 18

Salvation versus Holiness

Dear Brothers and Sisters in Christ,

As we grow in our walk with Christ, we come to realize that salvation and holiness are two different things. Salvation only requires us to confess our acceptance that Jesus Christ is our Lord and Savior and that he died for our sins. Once we make that confession, we receive the gift of salvation. It only took a confession. There was not much work involved. However, holiness is a lifetime commitment to live in the way that God would have us to live.

1 Peter 1:16 admonishes us to be holy because God is holy. God is putting a command on us to be holy. Holiness does not happen overnight. It happens over a lifetime. As we grow more in the knowledge of Christ and apply the word that we know into our daily lives the process of holiness begins. The Apostle Peter also tells us that we should add to our faith, virtue and to virtue knowledge and to knowledge temperance and to temperance, patience and to patience godliness (2 Peter 1:5-6) and the list continues. That takes work and an effort on our part to continue to grow in our Christian faith. If we want to be holy, we are going to have to do the work. We make the decision to no longer operate in the works of the flesh outlined in Galatians 5:19-21. We now resolve to walk by the statutes outlined in the bible to grow spiritually. The more we grow in our spiritual life the more holy we become. This a major difference from the confession of salvation. As a Christian salvation is the wonderful start on the road to holiness. Holiness is a lifetime commitment to live the life God has called each one of us to live.

Sincerely Yours

Write a letter to God thanking him for the free gift of salvation and how it has changed your life. Tell him how you are on the road to holiness and what you are doing to become more holy each day.

Scriptures to reference

2Peter 1:4-9, 1 Peter 1:16, Galatians 5:19-21

Date: _____

Dear God,

_____

_____

_____

_____

_____

_____

_____

_____

_____

_____

_____

_____

_____

DAY 19

Gethsemane Experience

Dear Brothers and Sisters in Christ,

We all know that God has a specific plan for our lives. Jeremiah told us of the plans God has for us, which is to give us a hope and a future. The plans he has for us will sometimes require us to lose friends and family members that we love to fulfill our purpose on this earth. These are the times when our faith is severely tested. As a Christian, I have found it easier to let vices and things go rather than the people we love. But on this journey, there will be times when we lose people we love. Our families and friends will not always understand or agree with the work God is doing in our lives. They may cut us off, betray us, deny us, or even scandalize our names. We should not be surprised. The same thing happened to Jesus. One of the 12 Apostles he chose betrayed him, one denied him, and the others deserted him during his time of adversity. They did not understand that Jesus came to fulfill a purpose and therefore could not handle it. So, they did what they did to preserve themselves. Jesus on the other hand was willing to follow the plans God had for his life. See he had to go to Gethsemane to pray and prepare himself for the hard task that lay before him. Destiny was calling and it did not look pretty but he had to stick with God. Sometimes we will find ourselves in a place where we are all alone to accomplish what God has called us to accomplish. Those times are the sorrowful times, but Gethsemane prepares us for our destinations in God. There will be several Gethsemane experiences, throughout our Christian walk. Even so, each experience brings us closer to fulfilling our assignment and finishing everything God has planned for us to do on this earth.

Stay in the plan my Friend

Write a letter to God about a time you felt sorrowful during your walk. Tell him how that Gethsemane experience has prepared you for what you are doing now in him. Declare that you will do his will just as Jesus did nevertheless.

Scriptures to reference

Jeremiah 29:11, Matthew 26:36-55

Date: _____

Dear God,

_____

_____

_____

_____

_____

_____

_____

_____

_____

_____

_____

_____

DAY 20

A Tried-and-True Weapon

Dear Brothers and Sisters in Christ,

Have you ever heard of a soldier going into a battle without knowing how to use his or her weapon? A dear brother in Christ who served in the military told me that you fight with the weapon you train with. A solider does not have time to fiddle around with a weapon he or she has never used during war. When the enemy comes, they have to be ready and the weapons they use must be tried and true.

If this is the case for fighting natural wars, should it not be the same for spiritual wars. One of the most powerful weapons we have is the sword of the spirit. The sword of the spirit is the word of God and if used properly our enemy will flee.

Jesus gives the perfect model of how to use the sword of the spirit in the book of Matthew chapter 4. Every time the enemy came at Jesus with a temptation, Jesus responded with the word of God and eventually the enemy left him. Did Jesus panic and start looking for a word to fight his enemy? No. He knew the word of God and he was ready. As Christians, we should make it a priority to learn the word of God. We should study it daily, so it becomes a part of us. When the word becomes a part of us, we will automatically use it when we see the enemy coming. There is no time to look for a word when the enemy comes. It is too late then, and we will lose. But if we study and practice using the word daily, we will know what to do when the enemy comes, just like the natural soldier. We are ready to use our weapon because it has been tried and true.

Be Courageous in the Lord

Write a letter to God telling him that you will make it a priority to learn how to use one of the most powerful weapons of warfare the sword of the spirit. Tell him that you plan to schedule to read the word every day and how you plan to implement it into your daily life. Let him know that you will have a ready word when the enemy comes.

Scriptures to reference

Matthew 4:3-11, Ephesians 6:17, Revelation 2:16, 2 Thessalonians 2:8

Date: _____

Dear God,

_____

_____

_____

_____

_____

_____

_____

_____

_____

_____

_____

_____

_____

_____

DAY 21

Thwarting the Thief

Dear Brothers and Sisters in Christ,

The bible tells us that the thief comes to kill, steal, and destroy. But Jesus came that we may have life and have it more abundantly. Satan's plan is to steal that abundant life. The bible tells us that Satan sinned from the beginning and that is why he was cast out of heaven. Once he was cast out his only job is to steal, kill and destroy everything God has for us and to land us in the fiery pit promised to the enemies of God. He has several strategies. He watches us. The scriptures let us know that he walks to and fro up and down the earth seeking those who he may devour. In other words, those who he may deceive. He watches us to find the weaknesses and vices that are familiar to us and comes up with a strategy to bring us to our own demise. In the meantime, he steals things of real value to us. He is a great deceiver because he is beautiful to look upon. The pitchfork, red suit and horns are a false image of Satan, and you better believe he is behind it. He is all about deception. Isaiah the prophet called Satan the son of the morning (Isaiah 14:12). The prophet Ezekiel describes Satan as the beautiful, anointed cherub covered with every precious stone and gold (Ezekiel 28:13). Could you imagine Eve when she saw his beauty. He said the things she needed to hear, and she was deceived. Have you ever been deceived by someone's good looks and enticing words? That is exactly what happened to Eve. Adam and Eve were driven out of the Garden of Eden by God for not following his instructions. Ultimately Satan stole the garden of provision from Eve and her husband Adam by his beauty and cunningness. The garden was of great value. He wants to do the same thing to us, and he is successful often. However, the good news is that if we follow the of the voice of the Holy Spirit living inside of us rather than the voice of our flesh (Satan appeals to our flesh), we will be victorious over Satan and his plan. Satan and his imps may make counsel together against us, but it will not stand because God is with us. We thwart the plans of the enemy by resisting the things he sends to tempt us and lead us astray. We resist the temptations that once ruled our flesh because we are now ruled by the Spirit of the Living God.

Serve the Lord with Gladness

Write a letter to God in which you release your authority over your life and give it to him. Let him know that whatever you have to deny your flesh you are willing to do so. Let him know that you will thwart the plans of the enemy by following after him and not after your senses.

Scriptures to reference

Genesis 3:1-24, Isaiah 14:12-15, Ezekiel 28:13-19, Matthew 6:13, Luke 4:13 Isaiah 8:10

Date: _____

Dear God,

_____

_____

_____

_____

_____

_____

_____

_____

_____

_____

_____

_____

DAY 22

Promises to Keep

Dear Brothers and Sisters in Christ,

Have you ever made a promise, and something happened that you couldn't keep it? Or has anyone ever made a promise to you and did not come through? I can answer yes to each question without doubting that I am correct. We as human beings make promises all the time. Sometimes we intend on carrying them out and other times we have no intention of keeping our promises. We made the promise because it appeared to be the right thing to do at that time.

Well, we can surely be glad that we have a God who keeps his promises. We can stand assured that whatever promises God makes he will make good on them. God wants to keep his promises to us we just need to live according to his will to receive them. His promises are in his word. If you believe and act according to his holy will, you will be blessed in all that you do. Psalms 1: 2-3 tells us that if we delight in the law of God that whatever we do shall prosper. That is a promise, and we can keep it if we are obedient. The scripture tells us that the promises of God are yes and amen and they are. We just commit to follow his instructions and everything we ask for according to his will, will be granted to us. Deuteronomy 28 outlines all the blessings that God has prepared for us if we are willing and obedient. Those requirements are relatively small in contrast to the blessings we will receive for being obedient to his word.

God is a promise keeper. He watches over his word to perform it. He wants to perform his word. We can keep his promises close to our hearts because they will come through. If we obey the words of God, speak the words and believe the words, we receive the promises of God. His promises are truly promises to keep.

Our God Comes Through

Write a letter to God thanking him for his promises. Tell him how you are willing to do what is necessary to obtain his promises. Plan your strategy for obtaining his blessings. Explain how you are going to study his word more, meditate in it and follow it so you can be prosperous on this earth.

Scripture references

Deuteronomy 28:1-14, Psalm 1:2-3, Jeremiah 1:12, 2 Corinthians 1:20

Date: _____

Dear God,

_____

_____

_____

_____

_____

_____

_____

_____

_____

_____

_____

_____

DAY 23

Words to Live By

Dear Brothers and Sisters in Christ,

Some of our elders have given us advice on how to live. Often, they give us words that they feel are good to live by or words that they live by. The words may be good or not so good, but either way we can look at their lives and see the fruit of the words that they live or have lived by. One popular saying of words that some live by, are to Trust no Man. This is a good saying, and it can help you get over in this natural world, but the bible tells us to let God be true and every man is a liar. The saying above tells us to trust no man, however it left out the part of letting God's word be true. We must be careful about the words that we let guide our lives because they may or may not be true. How many times have we heard a negative word (a lie), about ourselves and fulfilled that negative word in our lives? If we live by the words of God, we know that they are true, and the outcome will be good for us. In the book of Matthew 4 :4, Jesus tells Satan that it is written, man shall not live by bread alone, but by every word that proceeds from the mouth of God. The words of God in the bible are to be read, spoken, and preached. They are for us to put into practice every day of our lives. The Apostle Paul writes to Timothy that all scripture is written for reproof, for correction and instructions in righteous living (2Timothy 3:16-17). In other words, the word in the bible was written by the inspiration of God to help us live a righteous life. As a follower of Christ, we are not only to feed our flesh, but we are obligated to feed our spirits as well. How do we feed our spirits? We feed our spirits by reading the word and living by it. When we eat healthy food, we want to preserve our natural bodies, but when we eat spiritual food, which is the word of God, we can walk in health. The scripture says that the spirit of a man will sustain him in sickness. That is a word to live by because it is true. Jesus modeled the way to live by the word of God in his actions daily. We are called to do the same. Food is good for us, and it helps us to live, but the word of God is the word to live by. It is our guide to righteous living.

Feed Yourself with the Word of the God

Write a letter to God telling him about a lie you once lived. Let him know that you will now replace the lie you lived with the truth of his word. Write a plan on how you will live by the words from the mouth of the Living God.

Scriptures to reference

Deuteronomy 8:3, Matthew 4:4, 2Timothy 3:16-14, Proverbs 18;14,

2 Thessalonians 2:12

Date: _____

Dear God,

_____

_____

_____

_____

_____

_____

_____

_____

_____

_____

_____

_____

_____

DAY 24

No Room for Hate

Dear Brothers and Sisters in Christ,

Some of our brothers and sisters in Christ claim to love God, but they harbor racism in their hearts. Racism has its roots built on the foundation of hate. If we hate our brothers and sisters because of the color of their skin, we are not exhibiting Christ- like behavior. The bible tells us that if you hate your brother, you are a murderer. A murderer does not walk in love, they walk in hate which starts in their heart. If a murderer does not deal with his heart, he can commit murder. The bible tells us that God loved the world so much (meaning everyone), that he gave his only begotten son. Everyone is included in receiving the gift of God, which is our lord and savior Jesus Christ. No one is excluded. So why do we hate one another for something so trivial as skin. In Christ there is neither Jew nor Greek, we are all in the body of Christ. Out of one blood God made all nations. That makes it obvious that God regards us all the same. Through the death of Christ, the whole world has access to the good news, which is the word of God. There is no specific word for, the yellow, red, black or white. The word is the same for all. As a Christian we regard everyone the way that God does. That means that we love everyone, no matter their race.

We could be preachers, reverends, pastors and do all ministry work yet, if we hate our brothers and sisters then all of our work is in vain. We may as well stop doing ministry. The good news is that we can repent and ask God to remove the racism from our hearts. Repent means to go and sin no more. Get rid of the hatred and let love grow. God forgives but he is also a righteous judge who rewards everyone according to their works. We cannot afford to carry that seed of racism. No Christian wants to hear, depart from me you worker of iniquity I never knew you. Remember in Christ there is no hate. There is only love.

Be Free in Jesus

If you harbor racism in your heart, write an honest letter to God about it. Ask him to forgive you and teach you how to love. If you do not harbor racism in your heart write a letter to God telling him how you will pray for those who hate you and how you will love anyway with his help.

Scriptures to reference

1 John 3:15, Matthew 7:23, Acts 17:26, Galatians 3:28

Date: _____

Dear God,

_____

_____

_____

_____

_____

_____

_____

_____

_____

_____

_____

_____

DAY 25

The Reason for Heat

Dear Brothers and Sisters in Christ,

When trials and tribulations come our way, we often hear ourselves and others ask the question that has now become cliché, "Why me?" Then the response is, "Why not me?" Well, if we say we belong to God, we are to be purified as silver and gold. How is gold purified? Gold is purified in extreme heat. When it gets hot enough all the impurities in the gold rise to the surface. It is then that the goldsmith scrapes the impurities off the top. When the goldsmith can see clearly through the gold, he takes it off the heat because he knows it is pure gold. The reason for the heat in our lives is for us to see what is inside of us so we can give it to God. Once we take it to him, we can be cleansed. The hotter the fire the more impurities within us begin to rise to the surface. The more we go to God to cleanse us the more Christlike we become. We were all born in sin and shaped in iniquity (Psalm51:5). There are some things that we know about ourselves, but there are the hidden things that are unknown to us. Trials and adversity really show us what's inside of us. For instance, if someone is spitefully using us how do we respond. Do we retaliate, or do we pray for them? If we are still retaliating, we are not pure. If we are on the road driving and someone drives out in front of us, do we curse or do we praise God that we were not hurt? If we curse, we still have an impurity within.

Zechariah 13:9, tells us that God will refine us like silver and test us like gold and he will do it by fire. Fire in this sense is not the consuming fire that appeared amongst the Israelites. This fire is of a spiritual nature that tests us during various trials. When we go through this fire and stay on the course, no matter how hot the heat, we will come out like pure gold. God himself will call us his people. Your faith will be tested in this Christian walk. Peter said it best. The testing of our faith is more precious than gold.

God Be with You

Write a letter to God about a time you went through a fiery trial. Tell him what made you not waiver in your walk. In the letter include a list of spiritual tools that you will use to help you get through the fire.

Scriptures to reference

Zechariah 13, 1 Peter 1:7, Acts 14:22

Date: _____

Dear God,

_____

_____

_____

_____

_____

_____

_____

_____

_____

_____

_____

_____

_____

DAY 26

Faith and Work

Dear Brothers and Sisters in Christ,

The scripture faith without works is dead is a scripture that I have heard coming from the pulpit since I was a child. Now that I am an adult, it has not changed. Faith without works is dead is a scriptural staple that is the meat of several sermons on today. But how many of us can truly say that we know what it really means. In a previous letter, l I write to you that the words in the bible are words to live by. One may ask well how do I live by the scripture faith without works is dead?

In the book of, Mark (8:42-48), the woman with the issue of blood forced her way through a crowd to touch the hem of Jesus. She knew he could heal her, she just had to make the effort to get to him. She was willing to risk it all. In those days it was unlawful for women that bled to be out and amongst the people because they were considered unclean. It was her social responsibility to stay away from mainstream society. But this woman had to take the chance. Jesus was her only hope and she did what she had to do to gain her healing. This is what I call work. She did not care what she had to face to get her healing and her faith made her whole. In other words, she had faith that Jesus could heal her, and she did the necessary work to get the healing. Her faith was alive. There will be times in our lives that we are compelled to walk by faith. Walking by faith means to do the work of faith. You may be praying for a new job, a new house or to be delivered from an illness or iniquity and God can do those things. However, what are you doing to get the provisions God promised you. If God told you that he has a house for you, start packing and releasing the word that applies to that provision. If he promised you a job, start buying the clothes and preparing for the interviews. If you are sick in your body, identify the problem, speak the word over it and take the necessary steps to attain your healing. To work our faith, we first need to believe. Then we put action behind our belief and do what is necessary within our power to work towards the goal. Once we do the natural, God will do the supernatural and our faith will make us whole.

Work Your Faith

Write a letter to God about a promise that you are believing for. Explain to him how you are going to work your faith to gain the promise. Tell him what you are going to do to prepare for the provision because you know it is yours.

Scriptures to reference

Luke 8: 43-48, James 2: 14-26, Hebrews 11

Date: _____

Dear God,

_____

_____

_____

_____

_____

_____

_____

_____

_____

_____

_____

_____

DAY 27

A Note About Open Doors

Dear Brothers and Sisters in Christ,

Throughout our Christian walk there will be times of peace and blessings. These are the times when God opens doors that will ultimately change our lives. Even so, our enemy, Satan is not resting. He is looking for every opportunity to hinder our advancement in the kingdom of God. When Satan sees the blessings God has for us, he becomes enraged and begins to make counsel with the rulers of wickedness in high places to try and stop us from obtaining them. That is when we as Christians should trust God even the more.

Paul writes to the church of Corinth, that a door of effectual work was opened to him, but he had many adversaries (1 Corinthians 16:9). When a door of opportunity is open, be aware that the rulers of darkness are going to try and block it. I say try. They cannot stop us from getting the blessings of God unless we give up the fight of faith or just give up on receiving the promise altogether.

There have been times when opportunities for advancement were open to me. I must admit the opposition to my advancement was so great that I often ran or just gave up on the pursuit. As a youth in my walk with Christ, I was not aware of what was happening. But as we grow in Christ and become more knowledgeable of what this walk with God entails, we know that Satan never stops trying to tempt us. He puts oppositions in the path of the open door in hopes to tempt us to give up. But we need to hold fast to the profession of our faith and not give up just because the picture Satan puts before us is dim. We must trust God to fulfill what he said he would do. We do this by continuing to believe and take the necessary steps to advancement no matter what it looks like. We walk by faith and not by sight. The things we see are temporal and subject to change at any minute, but the unseen things are eternal. The promises of God are eternal. Therefore, we are to press on and fight the good fight of faith no matter what Satan throws in our way. The word says we will reap if we faint not. Faint not and obtain the blessing God has provided.

Never Give Up

Write a letter to God telling him that you trust him no matter what you see with your natural eyes. Tell him that you are willing to fight for the open doors he has put before you. Let him know that you will look beyond what the enemy presents to you and believe he will do what he says he will do for you.

Scriptures to reference

Date: _____

Dear God,

_____

_____

_____

_____

_____

_____

_____

_____

_____

_____

_____

_____

DAY 28

You Have the Power

Dear Brothers and Sisters in Christ,

We have the power to overcome all the power of the enemy. Often, we forget it and we just succumb to whatever the prince of this world presents to us. But God has given us the power to change the very atmosphere around us.

The bible tells us that whatever we loose on earth will be loosed in heaven and whatever we bind on earth will be bound in heaven (Matthew 18:18). That simply means that when we bind up a negative word, action, or demonic activity on the earth, it is bound up spiritually as well. All we do is use our God given power and it is done. The same thing goes for loosing things on the earth. If we loose peace within our surroundings, it will happen spiritually and naturally. The power is ours we only need to use it.

Talking about power, we can be reminded of Jesus cursing a fig tree because it did not bear fruit. He cursed the tree in the morning and by that evening it was completely withered from the roots (Mark 11:12-21). We have the same power because the Greater One lives in the inside of us. Jesus told the disciples to have faith in God (Mark 11: 22). As Christians if we believe what we say will happen, it will happen. Believing and knowing that we have power to change things allows us to walk in peace because we know we have what we say. If we look at the life of Jesus, there was never a time that he became victim to anyone or anything. As we continue in our faith we get to the point where we live in the power, he lived in. Jesus told the disciples that if anyone believes in him and the works that he does will do the same works, but their works will be greater (John14:12). We have the power. Jesus bound things, loosed things, blessed, and cursed things and every work he did came to pass. We have the same power he has. We only believe and put it to practice. We have the power.

Be Empowered in the Lord

Write a letter to God thanking him for the power he has given you. Explain how you are going to use your power to bind and loose things on this earth.

Scriptures to reference

Luke 10:19, Acts 1:8, Matthew 28:18, Mark 11:12-25

Date: _____

Dear God,

_____

_____

_____

_____

_____

_____

_____

_____

_____

_____

_____

_____

_____

_____

DAY 29

Are You Forgiven?

Dear Brothers and Sisters in Christ,

Can we truly love our enemies if we have not forgiven them? In our lifetimes it is a sure thing that someone will do something that upsets or hurts us. Oftentimes the response of the old non-renewed self is to hold a grudge, backbite, get even, or cut the person off altogether. We justify our actions towards these people because they have done us wrong. Yet as a born- again believer it is our duty to forgive. I say duty because God requires us to forgive anyone who has done us harm. Forgiving someone is easier said than done, but the consequences for not forgiving is a hard pill to swallow. The bible clearly tells us that if we do not forgive others for their sins that God will not forgive us of our sins. If we are not forgiven for our sins, we will give an account for them and receive the consequences for those sins.

That seems harsh but isn't unforgiveness harsh as well. I have done people wrong sometimes unintentionally. When I went back to apologize or tried to make amends, my actions were rejected. It made me feel small and overall bad inside. That is what unforgiveness does to the offender. We must forgive to free others from the guilt of their trespass, just as God forgives us. Once God forgives us he holds no record of it. That means we are to hold no record of the offense and move on as well.

The Apostle Peter asked Jesus how many times he should forgive someone for sinning against him. Jesus replied seventy times seven (Matthew 18:21-22). Now that is 490 times, but who is really going to keep count. If we kept count of how many times, we asked forgiveness from God we would be counting forever. So why not forgive others as freely as God forgives us? It is a guarantee that you will feel better because you will not be carrying the dead weight of the trespass someone has committed against you.

Forgive, give it to God and let it go. The bible tells us to cast our cares upon him because he cares for us (1 Peter 5:7).

Be Liberated in Him

Write a letter to God asking him to help you forgive others freely just as he has forgiven you. Tell him to guide you as you make it your duty to forgive others quickly and to keep no record of trespasses against you.

Scriptures to reference

Matthew 6:14-15, Matthew 18:21-22, Colossians 3:13, Mark 11:25

Date: _____

Dear God,

_____

_____

_____

_____

_____

_____

_____

_____

_____

_____

_____

_____

DAY 30

A Vision of Salvation

Dear Brothers and Sisters in Christ,

Write the vision and make it plain is a popular passage of scripture (Habakkuk 2:2). People use this scripture when writing business plans or plans for their lives and that is good. It is good because the word of God works when it is applied to our lives correctly. But I want to take the vision writing a step further. Why not write a vision for working out your soul salvation?

As Christians we need to take the time to write a vision for our spiritual growth. It can be done every year. When that year is over, we can reflect and see if we are working towards what we want to accomplish in our walk with Christ. The vision I am talking about has nothing to do with preaching, building a church or gaining wealth. What I am suggesting is that we sit down and write down how we plan to learn the biblical statutes and where we see ourselves at a specific time. We need to include a set time to read the word daily, how we plan to apply the biblical statutes to our daily lives and how we plan on accessing our growth. This vision should be between us and God. If we want to include an accountability partner to help us work out the vision, that is a wonderful idea as well. Even so it is of utmost importance that we begin writing spiritual visions for our lives. It seems that we are so focused on meeting natural goals that we forget about spiritual goals.

If we are going to worship God, we have to do it in spirit and in truth. Writing those spiritual goals will help us do just that. Just like we keep going back to our natural lists of goals we can go back to our spiritual lists of goals each day. I am not saying that we should write a book of our spiritual visions but if we are led to do that; there is a scripture for that is well. However, it is okay to start out with a scripture that we plan on working towards and work that out. As time progresses, God will give us more guidance on where we are to go next with our spiritual vision. We should just start somewhere. As the bible says at the end your vision will speak and not lie, though it tarry, wait for it, because it will surely come and not tarry.

Make your Vision Plain

Write a letter to God telling him the vision you have for working out your soul salvation. Add a scripture and explain how you plan to work towards fulfilling what that scripture says in your life.

Scriptures to reference

Habakkuk 2:2, Philippians 2:12, Jeremiah 30:2

Date: _____

Dear God,

_____

_____

_____

_____

_____

_____

_____

_____

_____

_____

_____

_____

_____

_____

_____

_____

NOTES

Printed in the United States
by Baker & Taylor Publisher Services